The Crossing Fee

IAIN BAMFORTH has worked as a hospital doctor in the American Hospital of Paris and the Australian outback, as urban and rural general practitioner, editor and lecturer, and more recently on community health projects in Indonesian Papua, the southern Philippines and other remote parts of south-east Asia. *The Crossing Fee* is his fifth book of poetry; he has also published a history of modern medicine as told through literature (*The Body in the Library*, Verso), and a collection of essays on European intellectual history (*The Good European*, Carcanet). He writes regularly for a number of periodicals including *Quadrant*, the *Times Literary Supplement* and the *British Journal of General Practice*, and has a column on culture, language and ideas in *PN Review*. His home, for the last fifteen years, has been on the French side of the Rhine but within hailing distance of Germany.

T0099107

Also by Iain Bamforth from Carcanet

Poetry

Sons and Pioneers
Open Workings
A Place in the World

Essays

The Good European

IAIN BAMFORTH

The Crossing Fee

CARCANET

First published in Great Britain in 2013 by
Carcanet Press Limited
Alliance House
Cross Street
Manchester M2 7AQ

www.carcanet.co.uk

Copyright © Iain Bamforth 2013

The right of Iain Bamforth to be identified as the author of this work
has been asserted by him in accordance with the
Copyright, Designs and Patents Act of 1988
All rights reserved

A CIP catalogue record for this book is available from the British Library

ISBN 978 1 84777 143 8

The publisher acknowledges financial assistance from Arts Council England

Typeset by XL Publishing Services, Tiverton
Printed and bound in England by SRP Ltd, Exeter

Contents

Psalm

I called out to you, from the root of the mountains,
from the mountains fallen in on themselves even unto Rotterdam,
where the very earth itself is of the nature of folding.
I called, out of my distress, and hoped to hear you
though circumstance closed upon me, with no place to stand
in the depths of the pit, in the region dark and deep.
The Alps saw and trembled, for even the mountains melt
when your wrath lies upon them, the fire gone before.

I wanted to break forth, and shout for joy, and sing psalms;
but you hid your face in the days of my affliction
lengthening now like shadows in the sere grass.
Ashes are the bread in my mouth. The nations are destitute.
And I am become a pelican of the wilderness;
I am as the philosopher's owl disengaged by dusk.

A Letdown

Venerable city, he called it,
and though he went far from Teviot Row
it would always be home –
the heart remembered by a lad of parts.

His northern circumstance, in all its flux.
Disembodied land of the mind,
it broke like a cloudburst on his plans
to walk the earth's low curves.

Why should the passage back be difficult?
Hadn't his father given him a map
so that he, eluding the past, might step
into the now-forever Land of Uz?

There were nettles at the gate
and in the great house a boy rehearsing
reasons for his lifelong trip
across the trapdoor of the mind.

Home was the House of Shaws, a place
of Gothic design and catastrophic
letdown. 'To set a stranger mounting
was to send him [   ] to his death.'

Night lengthens on his prospects
and those figures standing in the garden.
He has gone to live his calling
where only the irretrievable can be saved.

Victor Segalen

Anti-touriste de la terre-boule –
it would take another life
now the age of endeavour is synopsis
and history exploring epilogue

to find you in that navy uniform
at the missed death–bed encounter
(Gauguin in the Marquesas)
and recognise travelling for what it is.

'Space is rapt, the new conceptual rage.'
Enter it. Abandon the ocean
for the trek that calls itself China,
a relentless pilgrimage up the Yangtze.

Be seasick, even on horseback.
Write orphics with Debussy
and scorn that pimp of the exotic,
Loti, for his cheap effects.

Ease yourself now out of torpor,
alone in the forest at Brocéliande,
contemplating the not–you
and the book that couldn't be written.

Lenz

'A great era to be alive in,' he proclaimed,
climbed to the top of Strasbourg's sheerest Gothic,
then hung about Goethe like a bad critique;

posed for his silhouette, went mad in the Vosges,
got written off as dead a decade before he was,
went home to face his father's silent scorn;

tried to raise Friedericke's namesake from the dead,
was douched in a strapped seat for the mad;
took the pain of others into himself,

a pain so enormous he lost all sense of decorum
though recouped enough of it to play the fool at Weimar
where Privy Councillor G. cut him with contempt.

Memories of Holland

from the Dutch of Hendrik Marsman

Thinking of Holland
I see broad rivers
slowly chuntering
through endless lowlands,
rows of implausibly
airy poplars
standing like tall plumes
against the horizon;
and sunk in the unbounded
vastness of space
homesteads and boweries
dotted across the land,
copses, villages,
couchant towers,
churches and elm-trees,
bound in one great unity.
There the sky hangs low,
and steadily the sun
is smothered in a greyly
iridescent smirr,
and in every province
the voice of water
with its lapping disasters
is feared and hearkened.

¡Que Viva Mexico!

for M.S.

Keep your passport for 'the surrealist place par excellence' –
its chaos–politics a measure of its attractiveness
for artists tamed by Europe. On the 1929 Variétés world-map
it dominates the States: no government and hardly a state of its own
but every year it mounts the Theatre of Cruelty
and the Conquest happens all over again and guts you where you sit.
Here's where Eisenstein had to come to liberate himself
(judicially funded by his friend and benefactor Upton Sinclair)
from his belief in the revolutionary power of electricity.
Mesoamerica, the land for artists who need to say No.

So pin your poems on the cactus sprouting by the porch,
the bristly spines of succulent knowledge,
and leave a set of directions for our peyote specialist, Ambrose Bierce,
still disappearing into the Aztec calendar –
on his shoulder the black and red *oconenetl* bird
identified in Tlaxcala and of reputedly hallucinogenic flesh.

Luther's Fig-Tree

And the stars, they fell to earth
like figs toppled by the wind, figs green
and unseasonal, according to Luther. Fell with a thud
into my formative years. The revelation?

Adulthood would be a mundane, ordinary catastrophe
this side of Hobbes. I would war with
nature, if only my own. And never forget the story
of the barren fig-tree blasted by the Lord.

Or the other told by Ruskin, penning *Fors Clavigera*
in his Venice hotel. A quay peddler touting his ware – 'Fighiaie!' –
and the writer, moved by his sweet open face,
gave him three ha'pennies, not daring to touch the figs.

They were signs, a fruit so evil it couldn't be eaten,
'either in earth, or her heaven and sea.'

Promises, Promises

Words for the dark were what they put to bed
and waited till our heads had come undone.
                                    Then killed the light.

No stranger thing than what a parent said –
'Sleep, children, for tomorrow Christ may come.
                                    And grant us sight.'

Statistics and the Novel

Concluding is a consolation, wrote the vagabond philosopher;
then lost his mind. In vast regression to the mean
the classic bourgeois novel ends
in a conversion scene, and the death of pride.

Ear Eats Mouth

It's classic cartoon food
in the House of Deceit.
'Don't eat me;
eat my sign instead!'

Recognising the justness
of the call to universal peace
hundreds of assembled children
are tearing it to shreds.

Household Gods

Pottering around your half-timbered Alsatian house
I paused at the secretaire piled high with books
and took in the scene: the fat little baroque fetish-angel,
the Maria Mancini 'coffin' with its peaked pencils,
photos from Java, a postcard of *Rafflesia*
and another of Celan: „Schwerer werden. Leichter sein."

I smiled at your Esperantido twins *Inspirima & Terminata* –
requests (to whom?) to be filled with the starting-stuff
(a globaliser's tribute to the threshold) –
and thought: did you really abandon a stable career
for this will o' the wisp, this glimmer
on the post-millennial twilight veering into black?

I left you rueing the country doctor, a man who believed
poetry would bring him to his senses. Overnight.

Germany 1636

after Andreas Gryphius

We're done for, and still they aren't
                    done with us.
Europe's rank nations,
                    'trumpets exceeding loud';
blood-slicked swords
                    and the shrill siege-engine
have wasted everything once
                    husbanded in sweat.

The watchtowers are ablaze, the minster's
                    sunk into its nave,
the town hall ruined,
                    the big men chibbed,
girls gang-raped –
                    wherever we look
Fire & Plague & Death.
                    They take our breath away.

Our pavements are the runnels
                    for their butchery.
It was eighteen years ago
                    our rivers last ran clear;
now they're slick with people
                    squirming free.

And I can hardly bring myself to say
                    what torments me
more than the aforementioned
                    Fire & Plague & Death:
that so many souls end up
                    war spoil.

Skin Deep

Not the skin as a vast unfolded boundary
but your inwardness on view
in the prospect of mutual understanding.

Call it the unforced recognition of what you are
in the light of what I feel for you
(the flesh being ready but the spirit weak) –

the way one takes in the other's perspective,
unguarded in its giving, the outreach
of a palpable incarnate being.

Now, the whole body mounts to the face
unashamed, though anything but shameless –
our fever of signs must have started with a blush…

So tell me, love, you've been persuaded too
by that knowledge from the Garden:
there is no hiding place, least of all the body.

Turin

after Gottfried Benn

'I'm walking on worn-out soles,'
wrote this cosmic thinker
in his last letter. Then they haul him
back to Jena: REFER TO PSY.

I've no money for new books;
sit in the municipal libraries taking
notes. Then go buy cold cuts.
– Those are his Turin days.

Even as Europe's braying rich
flocked to Ascot and Longchamp
he hugged two dobbins in the street
until his landlord led him home.

Theogony

This is how Hesiod describes it, in his cosmogony:
Sky, Gap, Pit, Gloom, Night, the names that surround us,
the ground we walk on, harder than fact,
so that emptiness might come to fear for its very soul.

And the giant planet cools, and the rocks are no longer ardent,
and the world is the strangest naked place.
Stars fall into trenches, and in consideration of the matter
there are outdoor screenings for the adoring masses.

A century is born, and another, and another;
each with its unique digital identifier.
But the birds won't sing, and what the cities of the bulldozer era
get to see is the inside of a concrete block.

And humans are to be heard beseeching the gods:
give us the tools, and we'll do the job like centaurs
until the past becomes pregnant with the future, and the afterlife
is a glorious measureless expenditure of energy.

But the underworld makes evacuating noises like a drain
and nothing restores our monumental standing;
all those long goodbyes, whistles in the dark, beseechings
are a German tune, not Greek. 'Did I not learn and teach vacuity?'

Accelerating shortfalls, outgoings in pure waste.

Pyro Tyro

after Heine

The real reason for the Creation
I ought to admit straight out
hit me like an arsonist's
flushed fumble at his real vocation.

It's really so obvious! Illness
is creativity's root cause —
creating brings me peace of mind,
creating is the business!

Mediation and the Sunflower

Umbrella flowers from the Americas
are growing in the garden, a lithe composition
at each corner of the singed lawn.
Their yellow heads look down from a great height.

I might consider grasping one at its base,
and holding it over you like a sheltering parasol –
Picasso escorting Françoise Gilot
from the beach at Golfe-Juan to the dark room.

Instead we watch bees stream to their ritual centres,
the revelation being of a different order.
Light seeds a geometrical floret
whose very force is reciprocity, bold solar gold.

Anorexia

Simone Weil (1909–1943)

Like Hadewijch of Brabant long before her
what mattered in her life was love –
not devouring others, giving ourselves as food.
'He eats us; we think we eat Him.'

Love, it will rob us of our heart and mind
and make us die to ourselves –
although outrage at being asked to eat mere words
is the substance of our suffering.
Words satiate by demanding the most perfect No.
Then appetite returns, with a vengeance.

She urged suffering, without consolation,
in the prospect of a knowledge more terrible –
face to face with the connoisseurship
of God's rapacious, unconditional hunger.

Trauma Years

Speaking for myself, I too believe that humanity will win out in the long run;
I am only afraid that at the same time the world will have turned into one
vast hospital where everyone is everyone else's humane nurse.
— Goethe, 1787

It was Goethe who first expressed the hope
scribbled in a letter to his friend Herder
from a staging post in the Alps
that humanity might 'win out' in the end,
albeit at the cost of permanent nursing
and a landfill of sick-notes.

I've suffered it too, that dream of waking
to find the world is just one hospital
where everyone intones 'patiens quia aeternus'
and being staff means having to work
in order to pay off being a patient.

Writing there is for transactional ends,
and poems are a flabby metaphysical excuse
for the state that fails to keep the faith.

Robert Musil to his Critics

I'm inclined to answer, rather grandly perhaps,
as befits a Man without Qualities,
or at least a writer with an eye for exceptions:

a) new times are always, as it happens,
just beginning; b) any accessory
before the facts of life in its quantum-box
has already killed Schrödinger's cat;

c) in any case, prophets are inside-traders
in the bourse of finite events
and have to be right if they're not to be wrong.

An event enacts its accountancy or not at all.

Names and Numbers

At six o'clock, in the New Atlantis,
their heads are antic in the clouds
and both their feet in Gemini.
White-coated benevolent curators ask them
to stand up, among late shadows,
and leave their hotel rooms. 'Vacate them,'
they say, 'come be our understudies.'
'Come and have your bath.'

They shuffle to the shower-room
clothed in Leibniz's master heresy
of coagulated dazzling godhead
and dark silicon zeroes.
'Come,' they are told, 'cast off your liberty'
(although they renounced it
voluntarily, for absolute clarity's sake
in the gardens of pathology).

Clutching dependency to themselves
they stand on dignity, or gossip time away:
lame stories of their earlier
inmateship. Overwhelmed by nostalgia
they avoid the metaphysical divide –
obscurely fearing the flesh
and the torment of their neediness.
(They needle their carers with it too.)

'Go in, and be kind to them.
Ask them to claim what bears their names,
though the names are lost in Linnaeus
and an era peters out in disarray
with the introspective stories of the West –
no longer the fructifying pledge
of Adam in the garden, naming the beasts,
but the tyranny of numbers.'

Two Propositions about Time

What can we do for grief?
Grief goes on and on like the small
still voice after the fire,
mumbling to itself, in the original way.

Grief is weak and at a loss.
It doesn't know what to make of hope
refusing the very sense
it was thought to be hoping for.

It is a moiling in the heart
(not in its usual place);
it goes on living, wanting
us to remember too we only live

what grief says hope meant.

Quartz

You had to be a mining engineer to take the measure
of the German soul, its plummet and allure.
Kleist, Brentano, Tieck, Wackenroder –
they were all queuing up at the mouth of the abyss,
learning how to be roped down into the dark
refractive glacier heart. Boys dig, and become men;
and an underground cathedral swarms with tiny figures –
pilgrims, the remoter kind of explorers
who don't know exactly where they're headed
but know how they're going to feel when they get there.
It is merciless work, plundering consciousness
to let the mountain stray into their sleep –
the mountain made delectable with its abrupts
by laws as old as the backdrop universe.
Backwrenching too, with its buckets of burden,
and so many gone before them, polishing
the path, cradling the ore that grows in their palms
as they force open the stone laps.

One comes towards me quoting Jean Paul;
another asks me to follow, carefully, the inner edge,
where the centuries of rage have turned to petrified slag.
How long have I been standing here
in the vault of the mountain called Primal Suffering?
I recognise it by touch; and then I see the brothers,
Biblical men to a fault, sternly decorous
with their chin curtains and woolsack coats,
about to heave Joseph into the pit
in order to see what becomes of his dreams.

Buddha for the Born Again

Should we be joining them,
muscles and torsos
of the perfect body-cult
kneading the flesh
to a transcendent state
in every factory window?

Or pretend to be aseptic
engineers of the faux-virtues,
culture industry workers
lost in the tedium
of having to swallow
selfhood's old aqua-cult?

Body maintenance manuals
tell us how to starve;
we do, and call it 'plenitude'.
Consciousness is a token
of the limbic, and the unison
empty like God's mind.

Sympathy in Silver City

1

Broken Hill's roads were wide,
way too wide for walking on –
dark molten rivers of asphalt
in Australia's petroleum emptiness.

Fact is, they were chemical flats:
Oxide, Iodide, Chloride, Bromide (ours)
and the Trades Hall on Blende
Doors opened for us everywhere.

A sense of space came inside.
At night we studied the electrostatics
of lightning striking upwards,
and taking half the ground with it.

2

Streets away from the Sydney road
you could feel the telluric reverberations
of a hundred-ton trucking concept.
The earth was moving, and not necessarily for us.

Once in a blue moon, at the South Mine,
there would be a controlled underground explosion,
another attempt to shift the planet from its axis
before we woke in the morning.

3

Behind the Indian Pacific railway and Mario's Palace
the mullock hill of evacuated tailings had become a landmark.
Hundreds of man-years mantled with lichen.

Telephone from the Beyond

Here, the Dolomites crash down to the sea –
a vista of gorges, limestone bluffs and Roman waterworks –
and the simoom from Africa wrestles with the mistral
to parch the grasses of the Gulf of Genoa…

it's that pagan Mediterranean music Michelet heard at dawn;
the olive-tree thrusting its silver spears sunwards.

You don't even have to look to find him:
he'll be sitting at a café table, a glass of water in reach,
admiring the view of Europe's belvederes
and writing out a new dietetic regime to replace morality.

On the table that mobile incarnation the telephone –
the device he accused Wagner not just of using but of *being*.
The new Delphic Oracle is a slab of furniture
disturbing the peace. You'll smile to hear the waiter say:

'Monsieur, it's an enquiry from a Frau at Basle University
wanting to know the number of your pension plan.'

Viaticum

All those liminars, wayfarers, Christ-seekers,
tree-trunk embracers and Nordic walkers,
wending up the blue cone of a hill
on their way to the ultimate appointment –

has nobody thought to tell them
in some lean-to between now and Jerusalem
history is the exodus? They're set on a pilgrimage
although they're leaning too against the rain and sleet,

obvious as the modern self, in forward flight.
Hospitality demands we take them in
and impel them with assent. Walk with them a while.
Then attend to the absence in our hearts.

Baudelaire: The Ransom

To pay his ransom Man must work
with reason's iron implements
to clear and cultivate
two fields of pyroclastic rock;

to train the curtest rose out of the soil
or coax a single blade of wheat,
he has to tamp them down,
sweat on his brow, bleak Bible toil.

One field is Art; the other Love.
In order to propitiate
our *père sévère* on Judgement Day
the ransomed has to prove

that he can bring the harvest home
(O attic-avalanche of grain)
and cultivate a rose so rare it wins
reprieve from the seraphim.

An Old Film

An archaeological ocean rushes in on them
whoever they might have been in what wasn't wholly theirs:
French administrators counting the local dialect speakers
and listing them in generic Greek: *autochthones*.

Then the stampede of armies triumphant
and in retreat, a no-man's-land down through Europe
to where the credits run and Herzog
announces his next location: nineteenth-century Eocene.

Cinema: thought in uniform for the unaccommodated –
vagabonds living forever on the other side of the border
among the squat, teak, odiferous furniture
of Biedermeier postures and scientific attitudes.

The disaster to come squats in their stomachs
and won't come out, not on the way to Mesopotamia
or even as extras driving thole-pins in to house the marquee
for the captivation of their sad pale children.

Somewhere lurks Nosferatu, the great dictator.
Here, in the Rift Valley, a tattered poster to film geology
announces the dragging of the great ship out to sea.
First the last man. Then the first man framed.

Gospel Commentary Nightmare

You're at school again, reading some righteous American
on eating animals, and dumbfounded by the pornographic impressum:
the dark warm stink of Hell appears to be a rational farm

erected on the speculations of the learned Jeremias Drechsel:
one hundred thousand million damned souls
squashed into the confines of the German quadratura.

There must have been a mix-up in the incubator. The kindly
                                                    supervisor
turns down the latest baroque sermon on the tannoy
and gives you *De aeternitate considerationes* as bedtime reading.

Larval Elements

Friedrich Nietzsche on the earthquake in Nice, February 1887

Presaging catastrophe (himself
a living calamity),
the thought of the liberal world-order
deranged by massive
earth movements
cheered him – *comme gaillard*
touring Nice in the wee hours
to see where he could
smell the fear. 'We are living,'
he writes, 'in the interesting expectation
zugrunde zu gehn.' (As if
apocalypse, when it
comes, has always been at work,
except we call it progress...)
The inkpot danced its way
across the escritoire
while the narrow houses above him
screeched and rattled
like grounds in a coffee-grinder.
People slept outside,
flannelled against the cold:
it left him jaunty,
the only cheerful person
among masks and 'bleeding hearts'.

Voices. A glimmer through my lids. The clappers
churning the Angelus across at St Peter's.
Blather of bathers. 'Come on over here!' Others yell,
'No, this way instead!' Birds are billing. Jeanne as well.
Georges calls her. A cock crows. Up on the roof
tiles are being trowelled clean. A hoof
clops down the lane. A scythe hisses in the tall grass.
Knocks. Rumours. Masons treading overhead like navy brass.
Din of the port. The shriek of steam
from hot engine parts. A wind band's military theme
catches the breeze. Quayside hubbub. French voices. 'Bonjour.
Merci. Je vous en prie. Adieu.' It must be late now, you're
thinking; our garden robin has started to sing.
Far off I can hear hammers in the forge, their slack ring.
Water slaps stone. Steamers chug. A fly
comes in. And the sea, its planetary hue and cry.

Flaubert in Egypt

1

On the sands at Saqqara,
cocooned for eternity, the dead
await the end of the enigma.

Their cover has been blown;
tourists are invited
to finger the cracked bones,

strips of gauze, the material
life flown west
to the oasis at Farafra.

2

You climbed the blocks
of the unmantled pyramid
and stood aloft
at the limits of art.

Permanence isn't stone;
we live on only
in the signs we make –
the thing that's all wing.

Ode to the Potato

for my father

Who could cherish you, potato?
Dug from a valley in Peru
to be stacked in a cold
northern pantry, out of the way
of damp and light. But not,
eventually, of disregard –
that being the tribute rendered
to what we rely on most,
your lumpy, most conspicuously
misshapen vulgar body.

For you're the democratic crop –
earth-apple, common truffle.
Smuggled back to pious Europe;
set out in harrowed rows,
your mineral heart and rough
unpolished asteroid skin
did durable service as
the battery of Enlightenment;
convinced so many poets
only the utile is praiseworthy.

You kept the people hale
cramped in the dark with the other
smells, a rough approximation
of the conquered Inca –
pale dream-flowers risen
above Columbus's Exchange.
O stone turned nutrient,
your inner substance is salt
and scour, our very sustenance –
pabulum of the Christian faith.

A House in the Var

Plane-trees and alders and pines lean down at precipitous angle
from the scarp enveloping the village eastwards.
In summer their canopy makes the house as cool as a Roman villa
for dreamers on the balcony, in earshot of the river's
gluttonous way with sucking-stones. Every year we come back
and every year a different light pours out.
Pickles ferment in jars sealed the previous summer,
and summer itself is a lavender smell folded in the sheets.
Children's voices saraband around the corridors;
those younger selves straining to stay awake on the hammock
beneath the sugar spill of the Milky Way
and the bats' echo-guided drop raids on the river's insect-life.
I could find a line on the phenomenology of the house
and how (according to Gaston Bachelard) dwelling-places dream us.
Here it might just be true, in this house in the Var
dredged up from a Royal Navy assault on Toulon harbour
and demanding occupancy. One more heroic flight
levels out with the wasp's nest under the eaves and a view of tiles,
though this year we're scraping salt from the pipes,
caulking the lime plaster cistern, where Jeremiahs get to swim.

The Reef of Natural Causes

Everyone, it seems, is struck
by that muscular torso – Newton's;
one of Blake's three bogeys
sitting in his two-dimensional world.

Fewer note what he is sitting on:
the reef of natural causes,
a landscape made of tiny polyp
corpses, catacombs rimmed

with the most precarious fronds
of what the sea coughs up.
For the tides are always bringing
news of something strange.

An underwater forest of what exists
outside our sight, the silence
of Atlantis lost beneath the waves.
The colour of the sky is merest rumour.

Here, in the sea of time and space,
Newton's body extends its pose,
and his thought leaches substance from
the reef of natural causes.

He sits on a lung or some spare
body part, waiting to be
born into the fourfold vision,
the bed from which Albion must rise.

The Desert in Them

after Heine

A single solitary fir
on a northern mountain peak
drowses in a white mantle
of supercooled snow and ice.

Its dreams are of a palm tree
which, in its oriental erg,
mourns, quite alone and silent,
on a sterile Aeolian crag.

Blossom

after George Seferis

This body that hoped to germinate like a sapling
and bear fruit, to become the forest's ductile instrument,
has been banished to a thrumming hive
where monodic time is going to come and drive it crazy.

Midsummer on Shetland

When I came on furlough to the northern edge of Ptolemy's ecumene
there was day and twilight (no night to speak of)
so that walking on the dirt track from Quoys to Baltasound
we were moving through a world of soft contours,
everything nearly soundless, and the clouds dawdling
like woolpack into so many sleeping heads.
The faint glimmer of the lighthouse on this leafless coast
and the early warning geodesic dome
standing on its promontory over the parish of the sea,
the amber glow of the sound with its salmon farms and oyster beds,
were reminders, before the earth's brief stoppage,
of dreaming space abolished and Cold War eavesdropping;
even here, on this final island at the world's end,
data overburden is only an echo away, like the Atlantic heave
and the piped-in petrochemicals of the polar night.

Real Estate

Sometimes (less often now) we visit them,
the dear departed in their ghettoes,

row upon row of unfashionable Christian names
vandalised overnight or by slow effacement.

Soon enough the plot will be cleared
of our last traditionalists, decently shunned

and toxic now in their six-footers
who have, long since, been indifferent

to further neglect. We recall what pity
meant to those great Victorian philanthropists

who hired the master-builders of the Necropolis
before the angels curdled and Tolstoy

spoke his words of love and pity,
words that made Ezekiel's field quiver and

move… Hearts in our mouths, we move too,
on the level, singing small hosannas,

though where they're buried isn't the past
but the present's future options –

'descensus in cuniculi cavum' –
in the place they call the Netherzone.

Woodwork as an Act of Ostension

Father in his later years
turned his hand
to ways of mending things
that needed no words…

Stealing among his toolshed's
shavings and volatiles
I rediscovered the hobby-horse
that took its very first

faltering steps across
land and sea, into recondite
inkhorn French:

califourchon, turlutaine –
love-words up for stern adoption,
along with my own son's
                              dada.

At Mummelsee

My curiosity was roused too, to climb the Black Forest
at first light and observe the miraculous lake
lost in the mist of its own breath, our local version
of the sanctuary at Nemi: the earth's rind
puckering in the pitch of its stillness. Caustic limpidity
and pelty awesomeness of the meteorite crater
that works the modern mind like Symmes' Hole
the Victorian.
                           That would be my opening
to the centre of the earth: a hollow of unhousedness.

A journey like Dionysiodorus' in Pliny's *Natural History*
from his sociable grave to the depths of the Pacific
(with a return ticket to the world of the living).
There would be marvels to report: the weather in Japan,
corals as big as oak-trees, breadfruit from Batavia;
granularities, the great officina gentium.

How could I forget? Paradise has been locked and bolted
and the cherubim are in charge of security. Even
where Mnemosyne does hydrology.
                           Finding a stone,
I picked it up and hurled it into the dead centre
of the vitreous orb. *Weltraum*: a manifold
with blind spot, and the whole still open on the lee.

Cave-Diving in the Pacific

Showers of salt-spray burned my skin
as our paired oars smote and pocked the face of Nuapapu,
the white-capped outer reef's sea-wall
addressing Burke's sublime, its implacable brute thrust.

Then Friday (our man from Vava'u) boomed out a warning cry
as we neared the living rock. Lurching, spidering
thin air, *One World* tensed its ribs to crest the counterswell.
Under this ledge was Mariner's Cave, the grotto

Byron read about in a jack-tar story of the Friendly Islands
and made his blank heroic berg of no safe passage.
Rock of Ages clogged with time. What was I to make of it?
It might be a hole in the head, something Adam said

and lost to hermeneutics now as a surface of last scattering...
Less my weight, less my diver's fins and mask,
One World shuddered, fell and jounced;
and treading water, extemporising, I pedalled for the pitch.

'There!' pointed Friday. I stared at a dark underwater blemish
while water gnawed the oars. Extending his word
I took the plunge into sheer jagged wall.
My breath was a thread that pulled and tightened...

Sealed inside bossed rock, I plucked giant air
and saw behind me mercy's gap, the vertigo trail of light.
Taut and slack and taut again... It was breathing,
this stone lung, like something out of Pliny's natural history:

aerosol clearing to liquor as the sea sucked back
its tidal volume. Unsure of my place in the scheme of things
I made for the depths of that luminous aquarium
and saw, from beneath, *One World* treading on heaven's floor.

Mariner's Cave, Tonga

Lepidoptera

Alfred Russel Wallace, you forgot to
index the moths of Java Kini,
though you catalogued everything else
exhibiting life, from Borneo to Halmahera

beings so delicate they brush on the door
and beg to be pinned against the wall –

the eyeshadow dusted on the Dutch-wife bolster
where mouths had lately blundered,
its bulkiness as much a mountain of intent
as the lissome hills of Celebes

fickle creatures wrapped in gossamer
and guaranteed to self-expose –

now you can spy the eerie sight, in a room
blissed by the equatorial sun:
maculate hosts panting for succour
and their flail wings, broken and plundered.

Teacher's Day, Singapore

Europe, the children said, was something to do with history,
its surfeit product, along with languages;
such pompous governor-generals setting off for the task
of discovering innocence elsewhere, hearts full of stumbling blocks,

while China waits, basilisk in its logic. Here, things are in place
for the glee and whoop of what is meant by money –
angels serenading the lion in the honeyed tones of commerce
and the day of reckoning for ever postponed.

Empire now is the vestigial stoop of Victoria,
the sergeant-major's Salvation Army catechisms
worked into the president's address to the virtuous children.
They, workers of the future, are being roll-called on the assembly
floor.

Children who know their talents will be noticed only when needed;
incarnations of the market, smarter than the rest –
although smartness has been discounted by the workings of the same
and the myriad multiplying objects made sacred by desire…

For today, like every day, proclaims the dazibao, is a feast day
in this cantilevered city-state fabulous with its towers
that, from dawn to dusk, obscure the small imperial museum-libraries
to what is made, traded, treasured and discarded.

Flying Garuda over Java

On the early morning flight
from Jakarta to Surabaya
secure a seat at a starboard window.

Edge out of the night
and contemplate one of nature's
most sublime spectacles,

what Burke put in another dimension,
before the clouds throw themselves
together out of modesty

and constitute what Aldous Huxley
called 'white islands',
crags of volcanic condensation

(while trying to forget
Garuda's record of aviation
disasters and hardware problems –

Garuda waking
in an enamelled pavilion
high in the branches of the world-tree –

Garuda the serpent-destroyer,
whose wings when flying
chant the Veda).

These are the twenty cones of Java.
They could be those of Io,
mooning around Jupiter –

and a little farther away
Bromo and Semeru
swimming in their violet haze.

All of them sacred sites
on the most densely populated
island in the world,

caldera demanding appeasement
from the anger-managers –
even volcanoes want to live on surplus.

*

And the file of tourists
trudging through the sand seas
around the Tengger crater

to Lava View Lodge
and the lakes of turquoise sulphur
have to register their impact:

lotus-swimming nymphs,
Buddha smiling in his rotunda,
all the pavilions of our civilised acts

have been built cheek by jowl
with the natural terrors
we mean to escape.

Primal Unction

On a flight to one of the destitute islands off the Mindanao coast
my reader's hands were blackened by the fate
of the latest typhoon victims. In these ancient secular prayer-sheets
war spills only ink, and op-eds rehearse their indignation
between Wall Street and the sports pages.

In the poorer parts of the Philippines, the dailies are used as surgical
                                                          drapes.
Dried in the pantry to a degree below spontaneous combustion,
the murmur of disasters and good cheer stories
is tethered with clamps and folded, neatly, round the sterile area.
Necessity is the mother of invention. Who's the father?

When Jejomar Flores was dandled by the midwife as he came up
                                                          for air
the sodden front page of the *Philippine Star*
had stuck to his back. A spill of amniotic fluid had contrived
to render its banner 'TRUTH SHALL PREVAIL'
partly visible, in reverse blocktype, across his buttocks.

We applauded his entry into the atmosphere, his call for help.
Truly this child was an infant of semiotics.

The Crossing Fee

That was my passage to the other life:
snatches of cloud, scenes of the marine life at Tagbilaran –
'second-class component city' of the Philippines
and site of Legazpi's landfall and blood pact –
where I hoped to disembark and see for myself
the coral and bamboo church of Our Lady,
the Harvest Time Temple and serried Chocolate Hills
and in their riverine arena the tarsiers, those tiny primates
whose eyes bulge bigger than their brains.
Between sunrise and sunset, those blessed parts of the day,
I was shipped to the evidence of Hispanic endeavour
in the approximate centre of the archipelago.
First the prayer, and then the safety lesson;
or was it the other way around? Filipinos bursting into song
at the least pretext and usually in the wrong key
while the TV ticker tape told of another foetus abandoned
in a Manila street. I kept an eye on developments;
and on Shorty and Stumpy, my two Boholano guides
who would drive me through the barangays
to the other life, the relics of St Ignatius
and the evidence of polytheistic, polychromatic Christianity.
Now I could imagine all the dead resurrected
for Election Day, their terror and their need
to emerge from beneath the enormous banyan tree
and adjust their costumes before mounting the jeepney
that will convey their votes, with indecent haste,
to the spongy capital. Voices lifted, chanting
in a subtle psalmody, with spontaneous dog chorus.
Now I could see the island in its full splendour,
and it was childhood all over again to quit its living shore.
First I'd have to work out why the captain of the Cebu ferryboat
had sized me up, taken my pesos, then moved away.
I had no agenda for once, being interested only in company,
in the Japanese tourists next to me wearing tortoise hats.
And the sense of passage: to know what they mean,
the glittering rough cities, the temptation to exist
among figures waving on the Starlite Passenger Terminal –
'Your friendly & convenient haven away from home.'

Kite-Flyers of Cengkareng

From early April to late September,
when dry trade winds well up from the Java Sea,
masters of lift and drag in Cengkareng
(the shanties next to Soekarno-Hatta International Airport)
loose their dragons, dugongs and birds-of-paradise
in the face of a municipal restraining order
to protect the massive tonnage of the wide-bodied jets
coming in from Europe against the dusk.

The wind brings their voices, hundreds of small boys
on breeze blocks along the perimeter road
waiting for their fish to fly. Homemade plastic confections
or canvas on a bamboo frame break into sail;
swastikas in Sanskrit and severely Platonic geometries
slip the strictures of God's own legal system
and only nerves of gossamer, as the deep blue turns to indigo,
align such flying colours with the ground.

A last evening gust bites their kites, then lets them drop,
and already the Bay of Jakarta is swarming with signs
in the implacably performative script
of the global order, its steel and glass dirigibles.

Six o'Clock

Round it comes again, invariable, monolithic –
the tropics' hour of enchantment –
and the massiveness of the day in a hotel window
volatilises to the Somerset Maugham hour,
the first of the evening's gin slings.

What do I see? The 'villages' stood on end,
sleek in their lustred claddings
and the red roofs and minaret of the true kampong,
the Dutch church and its rows of war graves
which birds like coroners interrogate.

Behind them, the radio masts winking
neon from the skyscrapers around Plaza Indonesia
where the cool, marbled emporia
outdo heaven with their vaults,
floor after floor in gladed glass and steel.

My hotel's inner air is creased by fans.
Now amplified calls to prayer from the mosques
erected with desert money across the city
wail, out of phase, an idea of the day to come
that sounds like purest torment.

And I remember this was a city
built on a swamp, malarial till a century ago,
and no Shangri-La beneath the mansards
for its dollar-a-day survival experts
with one resource: the energy of expectation.

They live in lean-to bivouacs
and prowl the garbage heaps for new trends;
their knowledge of the living city
as intimate as that of their own bodies.
Waiters trundle out the discredited past...

Faithless, I bite the anaesthetic ice.

Docked Ships at Sunda Kelapa

for Richard Oh

There are many phinisi in the harbour
at Sunda Kelapa, high-prowed tall-masted Bugis schooners
floating on the surface of events.
Rimbaud would have seen them, docking with the Dutch army
in 1876,
stragglers of the South China Sea's
most sophisticated maritime traditionalists.

Red, white and green, their lateens
flutter above the faecal reverse-tide of the Ciliwung estuary
disgorging its sewage into the Java Sea.
Thus commerce and bodily exchange are brought together.

Adrift on the shifting two-thirds of the archipelago
with only the moon as escort,
these schooners have, for hundreds of years,
been leaning like aquatic trade-taxis into the wind, dispersing
and reuniting in small natural harbours
as far south as northern Australia.

So much history has gone into their upkeep.
That, and unwritten carpentry skills
preserved against modern lapses of memory.
And though you might tell me
it is the business of cutters, sloops and ketches
to 'disalienate' the several thousand islands of the archipelago
their true finality is to reach a port.

Base Matter

In Wanam there was the one river the colour of anthracite
and a smell straight out of the pickled-egg jar,
a warren of shops, gangways and a pub (the sign read 'Pap')
with its two *waria* owners offering sugary refreshment
and a mind-blow. The whole yawning village
rested on planks above the sludge, with ropes and ladders
descending to where the boats were tethered,
one marked 'Bintang Laut' and the other 'Polisi'.
This was a town subdued to its elements,
and they were one, and it was without radiance, being toxic.
Every fish in the sea seemed to be in the Chinese processing plant
back of town, ready to be dismantled and spirited away
for reassembly in another part of the planet;
the fish complacently waiting, in solid frozen blocks.
Walking there as one of the visiting party
I suddenly felt uncomfortable, almost ashamed
to be standing on the walls of Dis in this vortex of immensity.
And there was the treatment centre, with its benches
and two sickbeds, the only emergency care in any direction.
But who would be left to treat, when the land of mud
sucks everything into the sweet shared slime
of shiftless penultimate floors and landing stages,
and the world is an improvisation, where our feet might be?
The ferryman was waiting there, among such base matter,
ready to escort us back, if not to civilisation
at least to the district officers who spoke on our behalf,
though the sea had drained away, weighted by lunar indifference,
and left a vista of such stunningly featureless flatness
only laughter could absorb the infinite slippage.
Low tide, it seemed, in our world of excess and depletion.

Kiblat

Like the call to prayer, nowhere in the room lets us
forget where all belief must culminate:
the arrow to Mecca stencilled across the ceiling
or painted on the concrete floor,
a green decal clinging, in the better-class hotels,
to the bottom of the bedside drawer
(beneath the superseded *ecumene* of Gideon's Bible).
It points across the globe, from pole to pole,
to the granite house of Abraham
where millions trace the fulness of a circle
around the seething lump of meteorite
from before Adam and Eve's time – 'the sleep of ages'.
Sleep isn't an option, not for a mind
aware of how the rock, once gleaming white, has blackened
through exposure, they say, to our human stain.
It's the same kind of stone we carry in our head, an otolith:
the deep-ocean orientation system
holding us at the centre of every need and deed.
It will not allow belief to stall, for it has no hollow parts,
the circling around the cube that structures
space in all coordinates. At the centre of our lives
we find the desert sifted in our shoes,
fugitive in lush Sumatra
and God's name the pretext at every turn.

On the Language without a Copula

A language without a metaphysics – wasn't that
what Hobbes prescribed in his *Leviathan*?
The placing of names in linear order 'to signifie their Consequence'
and not our habitual copulative relation
between subject ego and predicate self, those rarefactions
of the verb 'to be' and grammatical illusion of an *Essence Abstract*…
And I'm using it, outside the charmed Vedic circle
in this mercantile language with bits of Sanskrit and Arabic
and crowd-sounds from a quay in Amsterdam:
signs, words, letters nailed to posters, Chinese encodings.
This was the great Asiatic secret of being at home in the world!
Safeguarding myself, I knelt at the worship-place,
aroused at the thought of language unbound for the coupling
in a patched room in earshot of the Java sea.
Afterwards, we could always walk out on ourselves, still
                                        uncommitted,
soaring free of plurality and gender too…
Whatever was lost would turn up later in tensed time.
Identity being what is given us, as well as what has yet to be.
Amid other agglutinations of the Word.

Ironwood

Anonymous, in the round, a black Asmat sculpture
lugged all the way back from the world's last nature island
to my living room. Carved from a single bole
six muscled men extend their arms and make the circle,
intoning, in the cipher-hum of the first day,
their vernacular anthropology, its pitch and cadence.
They might be a choir or a thunderstorm
or a bird of prey wheeling before the face of God.
Children have been playing this game for ever.
In its orbit of adoring predators the quarry is secure
and every warrior holds back from seizing
what the centre says is shared. It is fascinatingly empty.
In the House of Man, there is a spirit in every corner
and everybody – tangibly – is one of the family.

The Mud Volcano

In May, following on a small earthquake near Yogyakarta
on a scale common in Indonesia, where tremors of varying kinds
are recorded on an almost daily basis, and owing far more
in the intricate cascade of causes and responsibilities
(as informed opinion would later agree) to cavalier mining practices,
a drill bit piercing a mile down through a limestone dome
unleashed a torrent of sludge through the earth's old crust.

Thus began the mudflow saga of Sidoarjo. And soon the company
which for years had been stripping Kalimantan for coal
and shipping entire hills in vessels owned by its subsidiaries
to avid customers in all ports north of Manado
was in the mudpie business. But for all its media interests
there was no protocol for dealing with terror and silt
and soon people were thinking and talking the Endless Wave.

Lumpur: the glutton river miring everything in its path.
How were they going to account for it, the future urban planners
and road builders, when geology so patently had designs of its own?
When the great plates of Asia and Australia rub up on each other
and keep relocating things, unannounced, from place to place?
If all it takes is to find a loophole in the manual, and lahar oozes out
with all the slimy appeal and viscous density of concrete?

By November, political columnists were making the mudflow
an allegory of colossal administrative Indonesia, post-*reformasi*,
the disintegration of the body politic a loss of coherence
that began as a leak in the carapace of the geological upper layers;
and wherever attempts were made to shore it up with polders
this most anti-Platonic substance oozed out at every opportunity
in its determination to seek a new ground level.

By then the mud had dried, preserving the thousand footprints
of the villagers who crept back to rescue their possessions,
its imperious ridge mounting inch upon inch over walls and fences
until the red roofs were a flotilla, upturned in a sea of stupor.
The earth's inner turmoil was now a swampy smell.
And the dispossessed knelt like penitents on the thin hard crust
of effluvium that landfilled streets and left the buses waiting.

By December, the Ministry for Population Resettlement
was suggesting to the newspapers that the most expeditious way
to deal with the problem of the several thousand homeless Javan
                                                                families
would be to relocate them, with the help of modest cash incentives,
to the several thousand uninhabited islands of the archipelago,
thereby 'drinking water while diving', as the locals put it.
Besides, it was the way of things: what had been disaster would one day
be reconstituted republic, and no reason to dwell on the slurry

caked on faces or the undertow of lives engulfed a year ago.

On a Floating Island

Almost underwater at high tide on the Arafura Sea,
a vista of absolute flatness, waterlogged
by the medium that absorbs all footprints –
Kimaam Island, mentioned once by Captain Cook
on one of his journeys round the globe
and then forgotten to history, left to float on its tides
until it re-emerged under other names:
Fredrik Hendrik, Dolok, Yos Sudarso, Kolepom.

I marvelled at this place without firm footing, a netherland
of choking water hyacinths and mangroves,
shacks perched on stilts above the clumps of tuftgrass.
Then I remembered a word from Dante,
or Dante called up by Montale in the Cinque Terre:
trasognare, that alert dream state
in which nothing is tangible or knowable,
and all territory melts into the fermenting sea.

This whole island was sediment from the Digul,
which is to say: an atoll of the Flood.
And I was in a tent, sniffing for the salt breeze
or someone to soothe my distress, tortured by aloneness.
It was dark, in my sleep at the end of the universe.
Grand designs moved overhead like Laputa
until I emerged, smeared with insecticide and half an eye
on the crustaceans high and dry in the casuarinas.

I must have been a mirage too, for the locals,
a shimmer, a blow-in, another dispenser of dollars.
Mission radio cranked up for the next life,
pleading for uplift from imagination and all its works.
I watched the horizon recede into the dark
and the lights of a ship making for the Torres Strait –
on the edge of the world, in this rotting swamp
where an entire cosmology had foundered.

Iconography of the Early Philippine Church

With its bamboo walls, thatched roof and suspended bird cages
Baclayon's church of Our Lady of the Immaculate Conception was
                                                    for years
the redoubt of Spanish expansion in the archipelago;
then it became a miracle of coral stone cemented with egg white –
the million surplus yolks establishing the village's reputation for pastries.
Even the sun, that cosmic renegade, was searching in its immensity
for the hand that stirs, a compact with human sweat and spit.
Sundays, the Misa Baclayana hovers above the rooftops
and torments those of little faith with wild Augustinian freedoms,
the choir books being sung on Manila primetime.

What caught my eye, though, wasn't the ivory Christ on the cross
or statue of the Blessed Virgin fervently kissed by Catherine of
                                                    Aragon;
nor the books with carabao bindings and dusty cuadro paintings
and not even the gilded altar showing devotions under coconut-
                                                    palms.
I couldn't help but notice one of Nature's exaggerations had been
                                                    recruited
for special services: the baptismal font was a giant clam,
half of it at least, available for cosmic ablutions
and reveries of mythic feasting and carousing with the older gods,
much as Botticelli had imagined his Venus wafted ashore
to arouse love, mostly intellectual, and raise our minds to the Creator.

A giant clam that had opened wide around the time of the full moon;
a talkative mouth, as in Leonardo's fable, that in telling its tale
left itself at the mercy of the listener with designs.

Stranded Whale

From majesty to paper thin, Ida Bagus Rai's
Big-Fish-Eat-Little-Fish studies of the solitary *ikan paus*
that foundered a lifetime ago on the reef off Sanur...

It will be slaughtered at sunrise. A blue whale
conference-house-sized and a whole village clambering
out, with canoes and ladders and knives, to flense it.

And nothing will harrow its fathom-deep enfoldings
like the hemp and tackle of enormous death –
amputated flukes, bezoar droppings, spermaceti.

All are at work on the drowned explosion.
And time is pooling around each figure, man and woman,
for nobody knows the name of the beast is *sorrow*...

It expires on the beach where Bali's young warriors
step, row after row, into Dutch rifle fire.
Piling on top of each other to glimpse the cold black

shape of hysteria, the twentieth-century mechanics' drill.

Dawn in the Monkey Forest

All night, pawpaws and mangos –
large globular universals –
drop on the path.

Their lurid burst-split
feeds the monkey grammarians
at home in the trees:

linguists who keep me awake –
chanting proper names
in the registries of light.

Acknowledgements and Notes

Some of these poems have been previously published in the *British Journal of General Practice*, *New Walk*, *Parnassus*, *PN Review*, *Quadrant* and the *TLS*. The translation of Hendrik Marsman's poem 'Herinnering aan Holland' (1936) was commissioned by the Written World Project and broadcast on BBC Radio Scotland.

George Seferis's quatrain 'Touto to soma...' can be found in his *Tetradio Gymnasmaton* (*Book of Exercises*, 1940). Goethe's anticipation of the world turning 'into one big hospital where everyone is everyone else's humane nurse' occurs in the letter he wrote to Herder on 27 May 1787, indexed in his *Italienische Reise*. Nietzsche's comment on the earthquake in Nice in February 1887 can be found in a letter he wrote to Reinhart von Seydlitz on 24 February 1887. Victor Hugo's poem 'Fenêtres Ouvertes' is one of his late poems from the collection *L'art d'être grand-père* (1877). The Andreas Gryphius poem reimagined in 'Germany 1636' is his famous sonnet 'Tränen des Vaterlandes', a lament about the effects of the Thirty Years' War on the German–speaking lands. In contrast to the desperation of that poem, 'At Mummelsee' refers to an incident in Hans Jacob Christoffel von Grimmelshausen's famous picaresque novel of the same war when his hero Simplicius Simplicissimus climbs to a corrie in the northern Black Forest: the actual Mummelsee is only seventeen metres deep, but Grimmelshausen's hero discovers the lake to be part of a Platonic hydraulic system that transports him to the other side of the world. He becomes, in the twinkling of an eye, an orientalist. Mariner's Cave, a grotto with submarine access in the northern part of Tonga, referred to in Byron's long poem *The Island* and explored in 'Cave-Diving in the Pacific', is another artesian pore of this global hydrogeological system for vectoring ideas and experience.

Places referred to in the poems on the Philippines and Indonesia, including Indonesian Papua, can be found on a (good) world atlas. In 'The Mud Volcano' the expression 'drinking water while diving' is a literal translation of the Indonesian expression 'sambil menyelam minum air', which is idiomatically related to the English adage 'killing two birds with one stone': the mud flow disaster known as 'Lumpur Sidoarjo' ('Lusi' for short) occurred when I was in Indonesia in May 2006, engulfing the town of Sidoarjo and displacing the town's inhabitants. It is thought that the flow from what is now the biggest active mud volcano in the world will persist for another thirty years. Although contained by levees, adjacent areas continue to be swamped. The issue of drilling practice and liability is still being examined in the Indonesian courts.